Getting People To Visit

Your

Small Business Website

By:

Michael Kaltenbrunner

Michael Kaltenbrunner

TABLE OF CONTENTS

Introduction...5

Fast Tips for Increasing Visitors 8

Getting a Great Website 19
   Professionals Versus DIY 19

Checklist for a Great Website 23
   Easy Navigation..23
   Attractive Logo and Header........................24
   Side Bar..25
   Contact Details 26
   Offer an Opt-In...27
   Videos 28
   Your Blog 29
   "Squeeze" Pages..30
   Social Media 32

Going Mobile 33

Keeping People On Your Website 37
Domain Names..39

Getting Social..43

  Social Media...43

  Do Some Research.................................45

  Link Them Together...........................46

  Working with Other Sites.............47

  Make a Forum...48

Internet Marketing 101....................................50

  Paid Advertising..................................50

  Search Engine Optimization.......54

  Keywords...57

  Backlinks...58

Repeat Visitors...60

  Loyalty Schemes.................................62

  Free Shipping Offers.........................63

  Video Q&A Sessions...........................64

  Specials Days...64

  Blogging...69

  Video Creation.....................................71

  Articles...73

  Quantity As Well As Quality.......76

Sales Copy..78

Your Image..82

   Gaining Trust...82

   Get Involved...84

   Become an Authority.......................................85

Conclusion...86

INTRODUCTION

You might have a successful business, with a brand new website that cost you a fortune to make. None of that will matter much when there are no users visiting your site. This is a problem that many small business owners struggle with. Even websites that were previously going very well can start to lose traffic over time. How could that be? Trends with various online services, including search engines most importantly, cause shifts in who gets the biggest shares of web traffic.

Are you looking for great ways to get more people to visit your small business website? That is exactly what this book will teach you to do. You do not need to be a marketing guru to put these simple tips into action. There are plenty of ways to ensure that people go to your website, and you just need to learn how to utilize them properly.

Please keep in mind that there are no overnight fixes for a failing website. Even the most popular sites have some problems with visitor rates, and you can be sure they spend a great deal of time and money keeping things on track. The best way to implement the advice in this book is to take your time. Do things the right way, and stop looking for some magical solution, or quick fix. Over time, after you have properly completed all of the steps detailed in the following pages — you are sure to start seeing an increase in the number of people coming to your website.

When you learn how to drive more visitors to your business's website, you can start turning those people into paying customers. That is another helpful topic that is discussed in this book. After all, there is no point getting thousands of visits today, unless a good number of those people are converting into customers, right?

FAST TIPS FOR INCREASING VISITORS

If you want to get people to visit your small business website, read every chapter of this book. There is a lot of essential information here, and much of it is linked together in some way. Having said that, some people would like some fast tips that they can think about right now. Below is a list of many techniques that you can start to use *right now*, to bring in more web traffic to your site.

☐ Self-promote with your email list. People have signed up because they are interested in what you have to offer. Use that to direct people to things like your blog, your forum, your special offers, or other content that you have.

☐ Guest blog. You might have your own blog, but think about posting on the blogs of other people. It is a great way to introduce some cross-promotion, and make yourself look like an authority.

☐ Headlines are key. The headline is what people will probably see first, before anything else on your pages. Make sure that they are able to pique people's interest, but don't promise anything that you cannot provide.

- ☐ Promote your own links. In your content, be sure to mention other posts that people might find interesting, and provide a link.

- ☐ Start contributing to a popular website. You might do this for free, but it will help build more visitors to your own site.

- ☐ Optimize all of your content for SEO.

- ☐ Trade advertising space with other websites.

- ☐ Submit all of your content links to sites like Reddit.

- ☐ Talk about your loyal customers, including quotes.

- Use what works. If you have success with a strategy, don't try to change it so much that it stops working.

- Lose what doesn't work. It is easy to tell if an Internet marketing strategy is not working. Stop wasting your time on it quickly.

- Network. Build useful connections with other people in your industry. This is a cliched piece of advice, but it really does work.

- People love lists. Top 10 posts and similar things are extremely popular. Use lists as much as you can, without overdoing it.

- Have someone guest post. You can benefit from the following of a popular blogger, vlogger, or writer, simply by asking if they will create some guest content for your website. You might even return the favor, in order to convince them.

- ☐ Respond to comments. If someone posts a comment, don't ignore them. Never fail to reply as quickly as you are able.

- ☐ Answer questions on websites like Quora and Yahoo Answers. Make sure they are related to your industry.

- ☐ Response posts. Is there controversy around something that you have posted? Create a special post that addresses this.

- ☐ Use categories. This relates to good navigation on your website. Categories make it easy for people to quickly find what they are looking for.

- Write huge posts. These are commonly called "landmark" posts. Create long, highly authoritative posts that provide loads of great information. You don't need to do this too often.

- Always share your new content with social media sites like Facebook and Twitter. This will drive your followers to your website, and people will often re-share your links.

- Create content in all shapes and sizes.

- Upload fresh content as often as possible.

- Consider paying a professional to make new content for you.

- Consider hiring an SEO expert to improve the ranking of your website with search engines like Google.

- Find topics that are trending around the Internet, and use them when creating your own content.
- Never be afraid to pay to advertise your website, but ...
- You don't always need to spend money to increase traffic to your website.
- Learn the fundamentals of Internet marketing. It will be more than worth it in the end.
- Try using infographics with your website's link watermarked on them. These tend to get shared around quite rapidly.
- Upload videos to YouTube and Vimeo, with links to your website.

Getting People

- ☐ Make your own podcast to talk about your industry and help listeners.

- ☐ Turn your written content into video presentations and slideshows.

- ☐ Get involved in webinars, or host your own.

- ☐ If a particular post or video is popular, convert it into a range of different formats that you can upload.

- ☐ Don't be afraid to give links to other people's websites. They just might return the favor.

- ☐ If you want to encourage viewers to get more involved with your website, ask them to answer questions in the comment sections of your content.

- Add people on social media, because there is a chance that they will add you in return.
- Join social media groups for small businesses and Internet marketers.
- Turn your content into ebooks to give away to email list subscribers.
- Use SEO tools, even if you have to pay for them.
- Label your image files for SEO.
- Focus your efforts on people who are likely to share your link.
- "Piggyback" on the success of larger communities, and use them to increase traffic to your website.
- Analyze and archive statistics related to your web traffic. You might not know much about it, but you should always save it for later.

- People love images. For your links, use photographs, graphics, and illustrations to encourage people to visit your website.

- Use keyword research. Don't just randomly create pages. Learn to think like Google, and place keywords carefully in your content, tags, post descriptions, and links.

- Don't assume you know how the search engines work. Even if you do somehow find out, it might change tomorrow.

- Learn from successful people. There are lots of people who get more visitors every day than you could imagine. Listen to what they have to say, and learn how to adopt their techniques for your own website.

- ☐ Make your website look great.

- ☐ Make your website highly user-friendly.

- ☐ Ask your visitors to complete surveys, and get them involved.

- ☐ Link all of your social media accounts together, when possible, and incorporate them into your website and blog.

- ☐ Create an Internet marketing strategy and stick to it.

- ☐ Never give up!

GETTING A GREAT WEBSITE

PROFESSIONALS VERSUS DIY

As a small business owner, you might not have the funds available to pay a professional to build your website for you. There are other options available, and you can get some great results without spending too much. However, the best option for any business is to pay for a professionally created website.

If that is not an option, you might need to learn some added computer skills in order to create your own website. Luckily, there are a range of different services that allow you to create a great looking site, without needing to learn any coding or special skills.

One of the most popular platforms for creating websites is Wordpress, and it is highly recommended for the strategies outlined in this book. With it, you can just choose a template that you like and then customize it to suit what you need. There are a lot of great plugins that you can use to add extra features to your website, such as an online store, or a gallery of products and services.

In addition to cost and skill levels, you need to think about how much time you have to spare. It can take many hours, every day, to build up a popular website. Do you have enough free time to do that, while you are trying to run a successful business? It is important to remember that the topic of this book is one part of your business activities as a whole.

You will probably get to a certain point where you will need to pay someone else to maintain your Internet marketing plan. This could be one of your existing employees, or a new staff member who specializes in this type of thing. It is also a great idea to outsource the work to a freelance worker. This way, you can benefit from the skills and expertise that they offer, without the need to hire an additional employee.

CHECKLIST FOR A GREAT WEBSITE

You do not need to have a fancy looking website to get plenty of sales conversions with it. A great website needs to be easy to use, clean, memorable, and highly effective at turning visitors into sales. You can easily get something that does all of this.

Take a look at the following checklist of things that all small business websites should have:

EASY NAVIGATION

Once someone has visited your site, they better not have trouble searching for what they need. Don't make it hard for people to navigate through the different sections of your site, or you are likely to drive them to a competing website. Use a basic, functional menu that is usable from all of your pages. It is tempting to choose something flashy, but that is generally a mistake.

Do not use more links than you need to, because that will only create confusion. People hate making decisions about where they should go on a website. Lay the options out for them in a clean, concise menu.

ATTRACTIVE LOGO AND HEADER

You can keep these relatively simple, but make sure they look like a professional made them. Even if you cannot afford to pay someone to create the rest of your website, it is advisable to spend the money to have your logo and header created properly. Make sure that you fully utilize the logo, making it the key focus of your header image. This all comes down to branding, which is a whole other topic for marketing. If your own name is your brand, use that as the focus for the header.

SIDE BAR

In addition to a menu, which is often at the top of your pages, a side bar is an effective tool. These will show up on every page, out of the way of the main content. They should also be the persistent over every page. Use "sticky" links and information, which might not make good menu items, but are still important. You might include an "about us" link, as well as links to contact your customer service team. Any legal or technical information that you want to provide can be linked to from your side bars too.

CONTACT DETAILS

If people see that a business website does not contain any names, phone numbers, or an address, it can look pretty suspicious. You are running a business, so give people a way to get in touch with you. If you have a brick-and-mortar store, be sure that people can go and visit you without searching around for your location. Providing a map is another great idea.

OFFER AN OPT-IN

All businesses need some sort of "opt-in" offer on their website. This should provide a way for people to add their email, and possibly additional information, to your list. People probably won't want to sign up if you are not offering anything good in return. Giving away free ebooks is a wonderful technique to get people to sign up to your email list. You might also offer some sort of discount to people, or provide a series of helpful lessons to their email inbox, periodically.

Once you have a great opt-in offer worked out, make it easy to see. Don't hide it away at the bottom of your pages. Put it out there so that everyone who visits any page on your site will see it. On the other hand, you do not want to be too annoying with your opt-in offers. Avoid making them jump out at people, and seriously think twice before using any sort of pop ups. People learned to hate those years ago, and it is hard to use them effectively.

VIDEOS

There is no denying it: video content is *huge*. This topic is discussed in greater detail in the chapter "Content is King". Even if you don't want to use much video content for your marketing, you need to have one video at least.

YOUR BLOG

Sure, you might not know the first thing about blogs and blogging. If you want to get people to come to your business's website, and keep coming back, you need to have a blog. And it should be updated regularly with fresh content. Don't just re-hash the content from the rest of your website either, or there is not much motivation for people to read it.

You can hire someone to write your blog for you, or get a staff member who has a great personality. That is what blogging is all about really, and how it is different to other types of written content. Blog posts can be written in an informal way, and generally from a first person perspective. The posts can address a range of things that might not be appropriate to use for articles.

A blog can even take the form of video content, which would then make it a "vlog". People *love*vlogs, so it pays to consider creating one for you website.

"SQUEEZE" PAGES

These are the pages that focus on conversion the most. When someone reaches one of these pages, they should already be interested in becoming a paying customer. Your other content is used to convince them to buy your goods or services, but a great squeeze page is used to push them that last little bit.

A conversion focused page does not need to follow the same layout and formatting guidelines as the rest of your site. It should look unique, and make people aware that the time has come to decide whether or not they want to become a customer. However, make sure that people don't think they have been taken to a different site. If this happens, visitors might think they've been sent to an unrelated advertisement.

Your squeeze pages can be used to purely get people to sign up to your mailing list.

Once they have done that, you can send out your conversion focused content via email. This is a nice technique, since you know that people are already very interested in what you have to sell them.

SOCIAL MEDIA

Since social media is so vital to online marketing, as discussed in the chapter "Getting Social", you should integrate it with your website. It might be adequate to just include links to your social media accounts. However, there are different plugins and services that can fully integrate social networks into your webpage. This will allow people to do things such as following or liking your profiles, and even commented with their own social accounts.

GOING MOBILE

Is there a mobile version of your website? You might think that having a standard site is more than enough, but you would be very wrong. More and more people are using mobile devices to access the Internet. In fact, it is estimated that mobile devices will soon be more widespread than the Internet itself.

Consider the following scenario: someone is using their tablet or smartphone to search for information about a product. They are interested in eventually making a purchase, but they want to find the right business. With all of the wonderful techniques that you have learned in this book, your website is the first that they find. They decide to visit your page — and then there is a problem. For some reason your site does not display properly on their small screen. It either fails to load as it should, or navigating around your regular site proves to be far too irritating for them. And you have just lost yourself a potential customer, which means less income.

Your small business needs to have a website that works well on mobile devices. This is not an optional thing, so make sure that you are properly prepared for a range of different devices. It's not hard to do at all. Many website templates are made to be flexible, so they can work on screens of different sizes. Since it is such a simple thing to do, you cannot afford to miss out.

"Mobilegeddon"

Google has implemented a new algorithm that gives preference to mobile websites. This only happens when someone is using a smartphone to access the search engine. If your website is not set up for mobile users, you are not going to benefit from all the effort you put in to get more web traffic.

Are you still not convinced? Here are some more key reasons to have a mobile website:

- More than half of all Internet searches come from mobile devices.
- Mobile websites are faster to load than regular sites. Some people

don't have very powerful mobile devices, so don't force them to try and load a regular website.

▢ Mobile users are ready for action. For some reason, mobile users tend to be more willing to take action, according to a report from Google.

▢ Properly created mobile websites give an improved experience for mobile users.

KEEPING PEOPLE ON YOUR WEBSITE

Once you have gotten people to visit your website, make sure that you keep them there long enough to convert them into customers. Many people will leave a website soon after visiting it, if they find something that they don't like. If you can get people to stay on your site for a bit longer, the chance that they will look elsewhere will decrease greatly.

You can use the tips outlined in this book to make sure that people don't quickly click away from your site. Give them what that they want immediately, and never leave them wondering how they can find what they need.

Think about what really gets people's attention and holds onto it. Once you have initially brought people to your website, what will make them stay there? Is it something helpful and interesting? Will they want to look through all of the quality listings of your products or services? Whatever you have to offer on your website — make sure that it is presented so well, that no one will want to look at anything else.

DOMAIN NAMES

A domain name is the URL that people will use to visit your website. For example, yours might be:

www.mybusinesswebsite.com

This might seem unimportant, but it is one of the most crucial things in this entire book. Finding the perfect domain name can make or break your flow of web traffic. Choosing one is a relatively simple process, but the tricky part is doing it just right.

If you have a brand already, such as the name of your business, it might make sense to use that for your domain. So, if you owned a store called "Cheap Computers Chicago", you could choose:

www.cheapcomputerschicago.com

as your domain name. However, you don't necessarily have to use the name of your store as your domain.

Once you have chosen a domain name, think about buying up related ones. You could purchase the domains that end with different suffixes, like ".org" and ".net". This will make it more difficult for people to accidentally type in the wrong link, only to be taken to a different website, or an error page. You can set up these alternative domains so that they direct to your actual domain.

Here are some important tips for choosing a great domain for your small business website:

- ⬚ Make it simple. No one wants to try to remember a complex domain, full of different numbers and symbols.

- ⬚ Avoid hyphenation. You should not use a "-" in your domain, unless you have an extremely good reason for doing so.

- ⬚ Keep it easy to say. If you cannot speak your website's link to someone, and have them instantly know how they should write it — you need to think of something different.

- ⬚ Think about SEO. Try to choose a domain that includes important words for the search engines. If you sell shoes, you might want to include this word in your domain.

☐ Explain what you do. A good domain name will tell people what they will find on that website. "www.thebeststore.com" is a terrible domain, because that store might sell any number of things. "www.thebestshoestore.com" is a better choice.

Michael Kaltenbrunner

GETTING SOCIAL

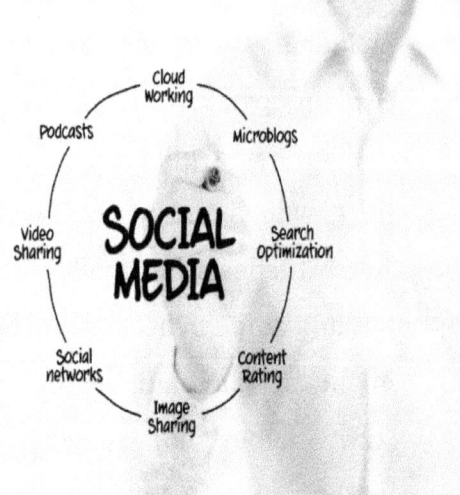

SOCIAL MEDIA

You might think that the computer age is slowly bringing and end to contact between businesses and their customers. You might be right to think so — if you were unaware of the popularity of social media. It is a phenomenon that has been steadily building up over the past decade or two.

Social media is not a fad.

At this point in its evolution, it is safe to assume that social media is not going away any time soon. Being pro-active with your business's social media presence is practically a necessity for modern marketing. Since the goal of this book is to teach small businesses to increase the traffic flow their websites, this is one of the most important topics in these pages.

Here are some excellent tips that you can use to implement a successful social media strategy for your website:

DO SOME RESEARCH

Marketing strategies are not successful by chance, and that is also true for social media strategies. Before you go and sign up to every social network that you can find, learn more about them. If you are trying to use your marketing resources efficiently, there's no point spreading your efforts too thin.

Some of the best social media networks for small businesses are Facebook, Twitter, LinkedIn, YouTube, Google+, Pinterest, and Quora. Even if you limit yourself to only these networks, you would have a very extensive social marketing reach.

If you are new to the world of social media, it is   important that you learn about how the difference services work. Don't make any assumptions, and try to figure out how people tend to interact within different networks. Your marketing content should appear genuine and professional, so you need to "speak the lingo" and understand how to use everything properly.

LINK THEM TOGETHER

You can link many different social media accounts together. It is easy to do, but some sites do not link to others. This will help to save you time, because you will not need to log into a whole range of different sites every time you create a new post.

WORKING WITH OTHER SITES

There is a lot of competition out there, but you do not have to consider everyone business your enemy. Try to think of ways that you can each benefit from working together. One of the simplest ways to do this is sharing each other's links.

It is probably best to work as a team with businesses that are not directly in competition with you. They might have offer related goods or services, but you each might fill specific niches.

You could also put together a special deal, where several small businesses unite to make a single offer. This often includes an item from each business, which goes toward creating a unique bundle of goods or services. Every one of the businesses will benefit from the publicity that is shared between each site. They will also enjoy more conversions, as people purchase the packages.

MAKE A FORUM

Building a forum for your website is a great way to get people involved in your company. You can provide a place for members to talk to each other about all things related to your industry. They can even form new friendships with each other, and use your forum as a place to network with new people.

A forum that is highly active can easily start to rank well in the search engines. In fact, some forums become the biggest drawing point of certain websites. The best part is that you do not need to create all of that extra content yourself. The members will make their own posts, and then more people will comment and start discussions. With very little effort, a successful forum can give you *loads* of extra pages for your website.

To create a forum, there are a range of different services and plugins. You do not need to build one from scratch, so there should be no coding involved. If you start to have a very popular forum, it might be worthwhile to hire someone to maintain it. You will need to be sure that people who post on your forum are not harassed by other members, so a moderator should regularly look through new posts, and deal with grievances.

INTERNET MARKETING 101

PAID ADVERTISING

If you have a good marketing budget, the easiest way to get more traffic is to pay for it. You might be spending money on newspaper ads or catalogs already. Think about how well those things are actually working. Are you seeing definite results? With Internet marketing, you can easily track how well your ads are doing, so you don't waste any money on ineffective campaigns. In addition, you can reach a far greater range and amount of people, 24 hours a day.

This is one of the Internet marketing techniques that is most like traditional advertising. You can pay other successful websites to display ads for your website, which will link to your own pages. There are also other methods, such as Google Adwords and other "pay per click" platforms.

With PPC (pay per click) advertising, you also pay to have your ads displayed. The difference is that you do not need to pay unless someone actually clicks your ad, and is then directed to your own webpage. This is a great way for small businesses to compete with the big companies who can afford flashy banner ads.

Google offers their own PPC advertising platform, called Google Adwords. You can pay to have your ads displayed on the search engine results pages, so that people who are looking for your niche will see them. In addition, you can get your ads onto relevant websites. This is a wonderful way to ensure that your advertisements are only being shown to people who are already interested in what you have to offer.

Facebook offers their own advertising options too. You can pay to have your posts shown to a greater number of people. If you are looking to get a huge amount of followers for your profile, but you just started with your social marketing, this is a nice option. Once you have lots of "likes", people will see that you are a serious business. It will then be easier to get even more likes, and so on. You can also choose to use regular PPC advertising on Facebook, which can direct people to your website.

Getting People

Michael Kaltenbrunner

SEARCH ENGINE OPTIMIZATION

SEO is all about boosting your website's ranking on popular search engines, like Google. This can be done by using certain keywords, and creating content that the search engines want to direct people to.

In days gone by, there were a whole bunch of little tricks that people could use to drive traffic to websites. This included simply stuffing keywords into content, or paying for a bunch of links back to a site. You need to be clear that these sorts of tricks are generally not going to work anymore. Search engines have gotten wise to these sorts of things. In fact, they have disliked them for a long time. It just wasn't until recently that technology became powerful enough to allow for algorithms that actively punished shady SEO techniques.

When someone is trying to find something online, they generally go straight to Google. They will type in what they are looking for, using keywords that they think will show them the best results. If you are searching for something, do you often scroll through every result that is presented? People usually only look at the top search engine results. Good SEO is all about ensuring that a website will be listed among the top results, for certain searches at least.

Proper SEO might seem like an alien concept to many people. If you really want to increase the amount of people who visit your website, it is essential that you do the job properly. Business owners might not have the time, or technical skills, to learn all about this themselves. There are luckily SEO experts who will work to boost your website's standings with the search engines.

Anyone who is serious about Internet marketing for their business (and that should be just about every business owner!) needs to have great SEO on their website. Otherwise, you are missing out on a huge amount of potential visitors.

KEYWORDS

A keyword might actually consist of more than one word, but it is still called a "keyword". Search engines use them when deciding the relevance of different websites and pages. You can find out what people are commonly typing into the search engines, and then use those keywords in your own SEO efforts. Just be sure that you don't "keyword stuff", or you will be punished by Google, and they will lower your rating.

Some keywords, like "games", are just about impossible to use successfully for a small business. They are just too popular, and there is loads of competition. Try to think of longer phrases, made up of three or more words. These are called "longtail" keywords.

BACKLINKS

Google looks at backlinks when deciding how well they are going to rank a website. If you have lots of people sharing links to your pages, it stands to reason that you probably have some great content. You can use this to boost your SEO. Not only will you get people visiting your site more from the links directly, but you will receive more traffic from search engine.

There are services that offer to sell backlinks to businesses. Do not use any of these services, because it is likely to cause more harm than good. You should only seek out genuine backlinks, from websites that are actually trustworthy.

REPEAT VISITORS

If you are trying to encourage people to pay for a service or product with your website, people do not generally just visit once and then hand over their money. The Internet allows the public to compare different companies in a way that was never possible in the past. They are likely to do some shopping around, check out what all the different competition has to offer, and then make a decision later.

Some users might even visit a website a number of times, before that actually take any action. This is especially true when they are thinking of making a particularly large purchase. There is even a correlation between how much something costs, and how long people are willing to spend researching their options.

Once you have done everything that it takes to get people to visit your website, over the competition, you need to hold onto them. What will happen if they visit once and then never return to make an actual purchase? What is the use of driving traffic to your site if they then leave forever?

Even if someone does make a purchase, you need to ensure that they will become a regular customer.

You cannot risk losing potential sales just because your website is not set up to create repeat visitors. Here are some essential tips for getting people to return to your website.

LOYALTY SCHEMES

People who tend to frequent your website should be rewarded, especially when they make regular purchases. You could offer special discounts for people after they have made spent a certain amount of money in your store.

You might provide unique discounts for people who have been signed up to your mailing list for a certain amount of time. You would be amazed at how many people are willing to spend a lot of money, simply because they were offered a relatively small discount or bonus offer.

FREE SHIPPING OFFERS

If you sell a product online, think about offering free shipping to return customers. This will even work if your prices are not the best around. When people see "free shipping" displayed one your website, they are proven to be more likely to make a purchase. Paying for shipping is one of the downsides of the Internet, so consumers are always looking for any way that they can avoid this added cost.

You might consider offering free shipping on your goods as a permanent thing. Once people realize that they can get free shipping at any time, they will probably begin to go to your website before looking anywhere else.

VIDEO Q&A SESSIONS

How about you offer a live video session, where people can actively discuss your product or service? You can demonstrate why your products are so great, and give people valuable information about how to use them. Don't use this as an opportunity to give everyone a big sales pitch. Provide useful information, from someone who really knows what they are talking about.

SPECIALS DAYS

Many stores run specials, where there are big discounts on different items, or even everything in the store. You can do that with a website. Make sure that you advertise your specials day, and send out news of the event to people who have signed up to your mailing list.

Michael Kaltenbrunner

Content is King

People want something valuable when they go online. This might be in the form of entertainment or knowledge, but they certainly expect it to be good. How can you provide these things on your pages? Content is one of the most important aspects of getting people to visit your website.

When you consider content on a small business website, it might be easy to think about sales copy and advertisements. Yes, those things do have a place in the process of making sales. But how many people want to visit a website just to read a bunch of pushy marketing content?

People are so eager for new content that they go out of their way to find it.

When the public goes on a hunt for some great content that relates to your business — you want to make sure that they end up going to your website. In order to attract new visitors, you will need to provide any number of the following things:

▢	Blog posts

- ⬚ Articles
- ⬚ FAQs
- ⬚ How-to guides
- ⬚ Videos
- ⬚ Podcasts
- ⬚ Infographics
- ⬚ Images
- ⬚ Discussions

"Wait a minute, I'm not trying to run an entertainment company!" you might be thinking. And you would be right, but no one is suggesting that you do anything that thousands of successful businesses are not already doing.

The truth is that if you want to attract visitors to your small business website — you need to give them some valuable content that they will actively seek out. If people are looking for something in a search engine, or they come across a link somewhere that interests them, it will direct traffic to whichever website it was published on. Do you want that to be *your* website? You had better learn the power of great content for marketing your business website online.

BLOGGING

As discussed earlier in this book, blogging is an important part of content creation for your website. It gives you a chance to interact with people in a less formal manner. Even if you do not think that you need a blog for your small business, you should still consider including one of your site.

Blogs are one of the most popular forms of content in the world. Any company without one risks looking out of date. Worse still, it might seem like you do not have the resources to put a blog together. You are a business owner and you know a lot about your industry. Show that to people by regularly posting to your own blog. It is a great way to slip some extra advertising in as well.

When you post to your blog, people will be more open to reading about your products. The personable sort of way that blogs can be written, seems to make people feel that they are not being marketed to. This all ties in with getting people to respect and trust your brand, which is discussed further in the chapter "Your Image".

VIDEO CREATION

Take a look at YouTube and see the incredible number of videos that are posted every day. Even if you hate Internet video content, it is pretty hard to escape it. People watch it on their computers at home and at work, they use their smartphones to view it on the bus, and they seem to be constantly doing so — wherever you go. From a marketing point of view, this is indicative of an absolutely *incredible* platform for business.

You don't have to be great on camera to make successful videos for your small business website. If you do decide to create some videos yourself, here are some tips that you should follow:

- ☐ Use a reasonably good video camera or smartphone camera
- ☐ Provide adequate lighting in your shots
- ☐ Script what you are going to say ahead of time
- ☐ Be friendly and confident
- ☐ Edit videos before posting them
- ☐ Always be willing to re-shoot mistakes
- ☐ Keep videos short and concise

Asking guests to do videos with you is a great way to add some variety. Think about your favorite talk shows. The hosts are pretty entertaining people, but you wouldn't want to watch the entire show if there was no one else on the screen. That's why they have guests and special appearances. It is the same for video content. Bring in other experts in your industry, or people who work for you. You can even include some of your satisfied customers.

ARTICLES

Articles are one of the oldest forms of marketing on the Internet. They were already around in printed media before anyone even had a computer, so it makes perfect sense that they would be present after the Internet revolution took place.

Some people have a misguided notion that no one reads any more. As the public is using computers and mobile devices more frequently, they are exposed to an even larger amount of written media than ever before. They write to each other in social networks, emails, texts, and in comments beneath posts. People are still happy to *read* the information that they want.

Utilize that power by creating a regular stream of articles to post on your website. The more useful written content that you have, the higher the chances are that people will come across your website through search engines and shared links.

You can even write articles to share with other websites, so that their visitors can see that you know your stuff. It is also customary to allow guest article writers to include a link to their own website, so that will boost your traffic even more.

If you are not much of a writer, you can pay people to do the work for you. This is a booming industry, and you can have very nice articles written for reasonable prices. Of course, you must pay a fair rate in order to get quality.

Make sure that your article content is full of helpful information. Teach people how to use your products in ways that they did not realize were possible. Give them advice about choosing the best items for what they need. In this way, you can essentially be marketing your goods and services to people — and they will not even realize it. Magazines and newspapers have been doing this sort of thing for generations, and you can now harness that power without spending a fortune for printed content.

QUANTITY AS WELL AS QUALITY

Top quality content is one of the most important things to include in your marketing. However, sites that have a lot of quality content will do even better than small sites. If you have just a handful of articles, and perhaps a blog post every week or so, do you think that will bring in lots of visitors? People are always searching for brand new content to sink their teeth into. There should be a new post on your website at least once per week, and that is where having a blog is a great option.

In addition to making people want to go to your website for new content, big websites do well in the search engines. Google ranks large, high quality sites very favorably. Having a ton of great content clearly demonstrates that your website is one of the best in your industry.

The old saying goes "quality over quantity", but you should be aiming for quality *and* quantity when creating content.

SALES COPY

Do you want your visitors to do a certain thing when they visit your small business website? You should! The whole point of creating a website for your business is to carefully convince people to spend money on what you are selling them.

You will not always be trying to sell something directly, and that is when it's best to use different types of content. There is still always a place for strong sales copy, not matter what you want people to do. This could relate to your squeeze pages, where you are trying to get people to finally spend some money. Also, the goal might be getting visitors to sign up to your email newsletter, or download your catalogs as a document.

Whatever you are trying to get people to do on your website — it is important to know the difference between great, and terrible, sales copy.

What is "sales copy" exactly? It is any text that is intended to persuade people to follow a specific action. Remember that part: action. You should already know *what* you want people to do, before you start writing your sales copy. There is no point simply listing a bunch of features that your product or service provides, or telling people all about your business. No one wants to read a bunch of seemingly random information. Believe it or not, but people want your sales copy to guide them.

Don't give people options, or they will become frustrated. Sales copy is not about outlining choices. You must guide people so that they convert. It really is that simple.

Writing great sales copy is one of the most important things that you could ever learn for your business. If you lack the skills to do it, hire someone to get the job done for you.

These are the key features of all good sales copy:

⬜ Clear. It needs to be easy to read and understand. Avoid using any complex jargon that might make people feel unintelligent.

- Engaging. Focus on what your visitors will gain from taking the action that you want.

- Concise. Keep it short! Less is certainly more when it comes to writing sales copy. If you want to keep people's attention, limit yourself to as few words as possible.

- Convincing. Sales copy must persuade people to take action.

You can judge how effective your sales copy is by how many conversions is leads to. Something might seem pushy or too narrow-minded. However, if it works — then it is *great* sales copy.

YOUR IMAGE

GAINING TRUST

Would you like to give money to a company that you don't trust? Most people need to have a certain level of trust before they will be willing to make a purchase. There are ways that you can improve public opinion of your business, and of you as an individual.

Connect with people on their level, so that they can see you are a regular person. While you should always remain professional, people love dealing with businesses that are made up of *individuals*. A big, faceless corporation is less likely to earn respect from certain people. Always deal with clients with respect, and they will in turn trust that you will do the right thing by them.

A big part of earning trust is having good online content. All of that information that you are providing to people will make people listen to what you have to say. When the public starts to come to you for answers, you will have gained their trust.

GET INVOLVED

Don't just take a passive stance with your business. If a customer has a question, you must always help them quickly. Never simply give a standard answer that does not solve their problem. Take the time to get involved in what your customers want, and they are likely to become return customers.

When you are online, participate in discussions, and use them as an opportunity to get people to visit your website. Don't just find discussions and then post a link to your site, because that is nothing more than spamming. Become involved and talk to people one-on-one. They will see that you know your business well, and it will help to build your image.

BECOME AN AUTHORITY

When someone becomes an authority figure in a particular industry, they almost don't need to market. Of course, you should always keep up with your marketing campaigns. If you can convince people that you are a leading expert in your industry, they won't want to do business with anyone else.

You can use all of the methods in the chapter "Content is King" to demonstrate your authority. You are more than a business owner — you are an expert, so act accordingly and make the world aware of this.

Michael Kaltenbrunner

CONCLUSION

As you can see, there is a whole lot to learn about getting people to visit your small business website. You do not need to master all the skills in this book, or use every single strategy. Try to find the things that will work best for your business. If something does not seem to be worth doing, consider giving it a miss. However, there are certain key techniques that you were made aware of while reading each chapter. If this book has suggested that you do something — it is in your best interest to do so.

For those who are still new to this whole Internet thing, please be patient. Remember that any good marketing plan takes time. You cannot expect to see an overnight increase in the amount of people who visit your website. Even the best SEO and Internet marketing experts in the world cannot get the job done instantly.

Have patience, be consistent — and good luck!

www.ingramcontent.com/pod-product-compliance
Lightning Source LLC
Chambersburg PA
CBHW070837180526
45168CB00002B/854